Photo Credit: Alice Teeple

Harvesting Darkness is Robin Morgan's eighth poetry collection, furthering a tonal arc begun with *A Hot January* and followed by her recent *Dark Matter*. She is a recipient of the U.S. National Endowment for the Arts Prize in Poetry as well as numerous other honors, and her work has been widely translated. She has also published four books of fiction, including the recent novel *Parallax*, and nine books of nonfiction on social justice issues, primarily feminism, plus her now-classic *Sisterhood* anthologies. An activist in the global Women's Movement for decades, recognized as a leading architect of U.S. feminism, and a former Editor-in-Chief of *Ms.* Magazine, she co-founded The Sisterhood Is Global Institute with the late Simone de Beauvoir and co-founded The Women's Media Center with Jane Fonda and Gloria Steinem.

www.RobinMorgan.net

@TheRobinMorgan

Also by Robin Morgan

Poetry
Dark Matter: New Poems
A Hot January: Poems 1996–1999
Upstairs in The Garden: Selected and New Poems
Depth Perception
Death Benefits
Lady of The Beasts
Monster

Fiction
Parallax
The Burning Time
Dry Your Smile
The Mer Child

Nonfiction
Fighting Words: A Toolkit for Combating The Religious Right
Saturday's Child: A Memoir
The Word of a Woman
The Demon Lover: The Roots of Terrorism
A Woman's Creed
The Anatomy of Freedom
Going Too Far

Anthologies (Compiled, Edited, and Introduced)
Sisterhood Is Forever
Sisterhood Is Global
Sisterhood Is Powerful
The New Woman (Co-Ed.)

HARVESTING DARKNESS

NEW POEMS 2019–2023

ROBIN MORGAN

We respectfully acknowledge the wisdom of Aboriginal and
Torres Strait Islander peoples and their custodianship of the
lands and waterways. The Countries on which Spinifex offices
are situated are Djiru, Bunurong and Wurundjeri, Wadawurrung,
Gundungarra and Noongar.

First published by Spinifex Press, 2023
Spinifex Press Pty Ltd
PO Box 200, Little River, VIC 3211, Australia
PO Box 105, Mission Beach, QLD 4852, Australia
511 Avenue of the Americas, Suite #K144, New York, NY 10011, USA
women@spinifexpress.com.au
www.spinifexpress.com.au

Copyright © Robin Morgan, 2019, 2021, 2023

The moral right of the author has been asserted.

All rights reserved. Without limiting the rights under copyright
reserved above, no part of this publication may be reproduced,
stored in or introduced into a retrieval system, or transmitted,
in any form or by any means (electronic, mechanical, photocopying,
recording or otherwise) without prior written permission of both
the copyright owner and the above publisher of the book.

Copying for educational purposes
Information in this book may be reproduced in whole or part for
study or training purposes, subject to acknowledgement of the source
and providing no commercial usage or sale of material occurs.
Where copies of part or whole of the book are made under part VB
of the Copyright Act, the law requires that prescribed procedures
be followed. For information contact the Copyright Agency Limited.

Acknowledgements:
'These Hands' and 'The Ringmaster's Desertion' were first published
in *Poetry and Writing*, in 2019 (online). 'Lacemakers' initially appeared
in *Columbia: A Journal of Literature and Art*, in 2021 (online).

Edited by Susan Hawthorne and Pauline Hopkins
Cover design by Deb Snibson
Typesetting by Helen Christie, Blue Wren Books
Typeset in Bembo
Printed in the USA

 A catalogue record for this
book is available from the
National Library of Australia

ISBN: 9781925950830 (paperback)
ISBN: 9781925950847 (ebook)

For Ursula K. Le Guin

Contents

HARVESTING
DARKNESS

I.
REAPING

These Hands

I study them by bedside lamplight:
An old woman's hands,
strong still but with a loosening grip;
bones delicate, gloved in blue embroidery's
prominent veins; skin spotted brown
as a hen's egg; nails clean, unpolished,
short for typing; fingers starting to stiffen,
curving to curl toward claws.

They twitch and tremor sometimes. Often
they cramp, drop teaspoons, fumble keys.
They've held a lot in their day—a newborn's feather-
weight and protest signs and bales of hay; stirred
soup and rallies; played chess, tricks, fair, Bach,
and for keeps: they've applauded, beckoned,
shaken themselves as fists; they've clasped a thousand
other hands, made lists, caressed the flesh of lovers.

They never presumed fingerprints were an identity,
lifelines a fate, though they did long to hold
the whole world in themselves, like the woman sang.
Once graceful, these now gnarled hands knot
and knit not wools but stories—grim tales at times:
a witch's hands. A child might fear such hands,
though they still twist in grief for other hands
that punch time-clocks, pray to the void for mercy,

pound gavels to muffle screams, pull triggers.
I study how to teach these hands to let go,
let it all go, let go now. But they reach past me,
grabbing pen and pad to scribble a message—
words I will find all but illegible once
these white-knuckle hours unclench to loose
this past cold light's gold dawn:
Hold fast. Hold tight. Hold on.

Self-Portrait of the Artist as a Bag Lady

Destroy what you would willingly dispel
at the beginning, from the very start.
Keep only what you're certain can compel.

Let go of anything that might repel
the sentimental or the faint-of-heart.
Destroy what you can willingly dispel.

Then, note details. Dead bud in torn lapel.
Flip-flops in snow. The ceaseless muttering. The wart.
Keep only what you know, what will compel.

Critics will do their damnedest to propel
you, friends will counsel you to play it smart.
Destroy what you would wilfully dispel.

Pursue divine dissatisfaction's hell,
ignore all others. Fill your broken cart
with only what you're certain dares compel.

There is no secret but to fail and fail
again lifelong, to be absorbed yet set apart.
Destroy what you can't willingly dispel.
Keep only what art's mirror must compel.

The Ringmaster's Desertion

I must lie down where all the ladders start
in the foul rag and bone shop of the heart
—'THE CIRCUS ANIMALS' DESERTION', WILLIAM BUTLER YEATS

My body gnarls around me now
as I excrete myself
calcifying to an exoskeleton,
a womb, home, shell, trap, carapace,
sanctuary, chrysalis, coffin. Why
the drive, then, to send these messages?

Does the snail long to be seen for itself?
Does the crustacean rattle
I am alive inside here? A rag
is ripped from some larger cloth. A bone
is a fragment of scaffold. A heart is just a muscle.
But my muscles have minds of their own:

I must hunch to gain perspective.
Only then, stooping high, dare I recognize
a creature arrayed in rag and bone who scuttles
across this intersection as the light
turns red, weaving, while laughing at the pain,
through the gridlocked traffic in my brain.

The Ceiling

Nights, I watch them up there on the ceiling,
till I grow dizzy and lie reeling
from their rhythmic pace, whispering
to myself as in a trance let it go let it flow
through your fingers like water like sand
like cool strands of hair when you run
your hands through it finally revealing
who actually moves there, so slow, on the ceiling.

It's a sign of the age, on this ceiling,
both my own and the one I'm now dealing
with. I imagine it comes with the territory,
though I swore I was finished with eulogies.
But if you outlast your friends, eulogies cluster,
making demands, crowding you,
spending what little time's left, peeling
away flaked excuses like paint from a ceiling.

What etiquette works to view such a ceiling?
Should I be reverent? Standing, or kneeling? No,
let it flow like cool strands of hair, water, sand through
your fingers, like shadow. Alive, each had a choice
to escape being broken or being untouched,
to feel deeply, or little, or nothing.
Now, an eternal field for unfeeling
is what they traverse: this blank ceiling.

...

So I study them there, each night on the ceiling,
tracing what it can possibly be that they're feeling.
They rarely look at me, eyes fixed
on each other's spines, a solemn procession.
When my turn comes, I prefer to walk
alone. Then again, likely one morning you'll find me
cold, silent, still, beyond any healing,
staring rapt, eyes open wide, at the ceiling.

Regret

After my time who knows what hells await.
Dystopias abound, and clocks run late
to spend those talents I so long misused
or squandered, assuming they'd crawl back, abused

but loyal, a cozy lap of purring poems
that, tame no more, scuffle through these ruins
leaving the stink of wet fur, snorts, growls,
blood trails on the floor. Something prowls

wild, out of sight, but I can hear it hiss:
Too many words to bear, too many lists.
A child lies starving, staring at you. *She* knows:
Too much poetry. Need needs prose.

Failed as a savior, misnamed as a poet,
I am a killing field. How can I still not know it?

Giverny in New York

(for Maria Nadotti)

At first it was all about light. Now shadow leaches
through the gleam on certain days. The critic
proclaims Monet's brush was made of light.
Young edges of his lily pond were clear:
water there, land here—viewing, we know where

we are in every frame. Then something shifts.
War. A wife's death. One son dying, another
gravely ill. Age. His cataracts grow so severe
he takes to numbering the tubes of paint to know
which colors he is using. Space loosens, edges blur.

How to know now where we are? The pond's edge?
Squinting down through haze? Or underwater,
blinking up ripples as we sink, Ophelian?
The canvasses grow panoramic, encircle rooms.
If denied detail, art demands scope.

Surfaces, meticulous once, now smear 'crusty'
or 'paint-free', the critic puzzles, unable to see
Monet now paints in braille. I also feel
my way to a garden darkening, not so
benign—his subjects becoming mine. Mute violence

utters how plants competing for space and sun
cheer the tree's suffering an amputated limb. Mosquitos
stab skins, bloat on blood; dragonflies prey on mosquitos;
pigeons bully finches at the feeders and a red-tailed hawk
snaps up a pigeon, mid-dive, in a shriek of feathers,

while dried froth wreathes the fly-sequined tongue of a mouse
I poisoned. How does your garden grow? The world
in miniature: beauty, hunger, murder, art driven to
abstraction. I must number my syllables before I fail
to recall which words can translate this from braille.

The Taxidermist

She wore open-toed alligator shoes,
swung a python-skin purse.

She stuffed the child skillfully.
To keep. To hold. To treasure. To display.

Small fluffy ermine eternally
in mid-snarl, the child

was so packed with her love
it was doomed forever

to lack even the peace of being
forgotten. The child lived

skinned, stripped, ignorant,
hollowed of everything but

that old poisonous gas
its creator called love,

well aware such a creature
this life-like would be

all the buzz, in demand
by collectors.

And, gathering dust,
so I was. So I was.

'The Fish'

(In memoriam Elizabeth Bishop)

Each time certain this time you're done for,
freefall through scorched air you fly
to be caught again, killed again, saved
and left living, for somebody's whimsical why.

Each suffering hooks you, tugs
your entire unbearable weight through your lip
till you're one pure pain, light sears your sight
your gills gasp fire as you swing arc drop

stunned somewhere hard. Then a face
studies your spasms as you convulse,
admires five old snapped lines grown
into your flesh where you got away and away and away—

and the face lets the fish go, since you're braver
than death. And she's certain she's done you a favor.

The Will

My latter years crisp inward—frail leaves
of autumn, tawny, glowing with translucence,
loath to release and flutter free-fall in a breeze
of abandon, purchased dearly with nonsentience.
The world's insane as always. But I'm done
with planning   except perhaps a final gesture
to plot your safety, protect you when I'm gone,
aware poems are my real divestiture,
last words on a page, a babble few long
to comprehend: a simile maternal and vestigial,
metaphor's sting blunted by an ancient tongue,
best understood by far in the original.
While you, wise child, are under no such obligation.
You chose an art that needed no translation.

Pearls

She slept naked sometimes, wearing only pearls,
stared in the mirror at her weathered face and smiled,
brushed silver hair grown back post-chemo as white curls—
but noticed something in the eyes: obsessive, wild

with pain as an oyster frantic to wrap the wound
gouged raw by sand grains pour its tender flesh,
internal bandage self on self, winding round
to layer smooth agony's sharp edge

toward satin iridescent art. A parrotfish
chews reef, gnaws rock, searches for algae, digests
this into fine white sand, crystals of which
will madden the oyster once they are the oyster's guest.

Some oysters escape harvesting and sink
to the seabed—wound and all—where parrotfish
seek their prey. But unworn pearls grow dim,
needing warmth and oil to satisfy the itch,

a skin to graze, a pulsing heart.
She sleeps naked, wearing pearls, to play her part.

II.
THRESHING

An Idea of Disorder

(for Alida Brill)

No matter how you try
you'll make a mess of it.
We all do. Entropy
rules the known universe.

Known. There's the rub:
our curiosity, our thirst
for some dimension where
the work might be perfected,

love mature unscarred,
each moment realized.
An idea of order complete
as that, though, might descend

arrogant as an angel
upsetting our readiness
to scrutinize our tragedies
and take a tyrant's charge—

sweep our spilled sins
out, mop up our blood,
and bury what we began.
No matter what your plan,

praise its flaws—for fear
that entropy itself
might shape its own divinity
and outlive its end's end.

...

No matter how you try
it makes a mess of you.
So trust disorder's order,
be glad all permanence

is temporary, since
no matter what you lose
you gain: chaos composts
grief and love together. Live,

then, as if you never knew
the last act always ends
with bodies on the floor
and Fortinbras at the door.

The Wager

Not at the last but at the very last.

—FRANZ KAFKA

Not yet the finish, not the last
stand. But near the penultimate, the last
hope—though far enough from the last
chance. That is, if one can last.

Not like the moment I said that last
goodbye on the street, not knowing I'd outlast
him. Not like the one look back from her, that last
glance at me before boarding her plane at last.

Not like the loves that would surely always last
and were never meant to linger, much less last.
Yet who would dare this risk called living, at the last,
if not for betting on that very last?

Terms of Art

(for Cherríe Moraga)

Some people, they claim, manage to die
peacefully in their sleep. How
can anyone tell that? How does anyone say
how anyone lives or could die—above all
in their sleep? For in that sleep who knows

what wakenings may come? The mystery slams shut
and locks behind you once you enter it. Only the one
question—what now?—endures. No matter
how you answer that, you're dead. Nyctophobia is fear
of darkness, octophobia fear of light. Terms of art.

The best you can long for and dread is to live
out your life as an artist, I'm betting. Preoccupied? Yes.
Arrogant? Certainly. Fools snarl, "Elitist,"—as if
this didn't demand obsession driving its relentless
harrow across your lifework's form, plus pitiless

indifference to the cries of those who dared believe
you loved them—and so you did, for rare moments
wedged between or at
the edge of magic, when dailiness was not
irrelevant, not trivial and tortuous like need.
But that required *will*, your will to choose

love of darkness or of light, the will
to select one aim above all others, to bend every
action you thereafter take toward that sole end
to which each string of your existence
vibrates, the worst you dread and long for, the life

you chose. Who cares how you will die? Some aneurism
might bloom inside your skull, cascading perfection
you'd once crawled through days and thrashed through nights
to find: that rupture beyond peace, unprofanable—only to laugh
at the last, because it was never attainable.

Elegy for a Husband

Here at this tolling of the midnight bell
when silence is most reverent and rapt,
your death certificate lies flatline all
before me, no longer an imaginary draft.

Subdural hematoma, blow to the head.
Quick, at least—the slip, the fall, the big bang.
We'd said goodbye years earlier.
Years before that, I'd stripped off your ring.

You had the tools of poetry,
I was a jewel in the rough
hunched at your feet inhaling technique
and paying for that with my youth.

After the cruelties bestowed by you
and me on me and you, after the autopsy
of them into our verse, I can confess
I took my joy in it: building resurrection

from decay, raising the dead, claiming
what was lost and making it mine—once
I'd made it mine. I remember, though, the rooftop
where I came to jump, but stayed to dance.

Still, I've outlived you. Odd, to feel so free.
Though to this day I swear I cannot tell
what drew and held me
there so long: the suffering or the skill.

A Sighting

(for Janita Maria)

Beautiful, scarred, brave, timorous,
young vegetarian omnivorous
to learn the whole of things, you spied it. We froze,
garden statues but for the glance our gaze
exchanged confirming the iridescent blur
was real: in a city backyard, wings awhirr,
a ruby-throated hummingbird. Hush, I thought,
some other day teach how that furnace heart
pounds 1200 beats a minute, that beak
can suck a meadow dry of sweetness, stake
then stab a rival's breast until the other
wears blood-ruby beads wet on each tiny feather.
You were radiant as it drained the trumpet vine.
Again, I was glad I'm in your life, and you in mine.

The Frequency

Federal prosecutors in Brazil opened an investigation into a reported massacre of 10 members of an uncontacted Indigenous tribe gathering eggs along the river in a remote part of the Amazon, where the tribe encountered gold miners. The miners bragged about the killings and about cutting up the bodies and throwing them in the river. Funding has been drastically cut for Indigenous Affairs, despite recent and continuing intrusions, which activists say amounts to genocide.

(BASED ON A REPORT IN *THE NEW YORK TIMES*, SEPTEMBER, 2017)

1.
Back from the dead, here you are again,
this time your reach exceeding your grasp,
trying your most but not always your best.
Blame the frequency.

A low-level frequency you don't even notice
till you stumble across it when otherwise
focused renewing your license to practice poetry.
And there it is. There it's been all along.

Soft, subtle, stealthy, a never-off motor
once you're awake, oscillating between
3 Hertz and 7: part of you always in shudder.

And why not? Some other universe may
permit stillness, but might cost
you too high a price: poetry.
Here, we shudder in terror when seeing

the truth of ourselves, tremble
awestruck at the beauty—
our disease a propensity for metaphor
that shakes us to the mortal core.

2.

When tourists float the Amazon
what's left of native peoples sometime
stand, small clusters between three and seven,
on the banks. The women shout *"Pishtaco"*—

which means "evil strangers who come
to steal our oil." Translated,
this strikes the tourists as a protest against
mining for natural resources.

Which is true, partly: slashed–and–burnt jungle
—agribusiness now—feeds cattle, yields soy.
Mining sends minerals to China.
One tribe in Brazil, the Akuntsu, has only four

members alive. Near them, The Man of the Hole
as anthropologists call him, lives
in a hollow in the floor of the jungle, firing
arrows if approached. He's the last of his tribe.

It's accurate, then, what the tourists think,
just not the way tourists think it.
The term *pishtaco* comes from the 16th century
when Spanish *conquistadores* explored

the Amazon and found to their frustration
how humidity quickly flaked
their muskets into rust. Inventive men,
devoted to their Christ, they simply killed

the natives, boiled the coppery bodies
in iron pots, and used the rendered fat
to grease their weapons:
Pishtaco.

3.
The frequency never ceases
but we adapt to it, we ignore it. Unnatural
resources become normal. What practicing
poetry spoils you for grasping, though,

is how each of us in this dark universe has not
wakened more frequently to just such a frequency,
how we are each of us not in unceasing shudder at
what   we   are,

not one seizure of grief after another, not convulsed
with mourning, shivering from cold
blood oozing sluggish along rusted hearts, not
cramped by sorrow, spastic with fear.

Back from the dead again, here you are,
trying your best. *This* universe,
this terminal health some call metaphor,
trembling with dread at the price of a poem.

Dig while you can, I translate. *Dig. Dig deeper.*
Then hide and wait. Wait. Force yourself to survive.
Fire poems when strangers approach you.
You might be the last of your tribe.

Lacemakers

(for Suzanne Braun Levine)

The little Infanta Princess of Spain
was dressed in lace for her portrait.
Yet courtiers thought her not perfect enough,
so added the Dwarf to heighten her beauty.
    The painting is famous because of the Dwarf.

They also assumed it our duty for centuries
to gladly go blind tatting the edges
of their nightcaps, cuffs, wedding hems,
petticoats, kerchiefs, and veils,
    all without flaws, without even one—not one—flaw.

They never perceived our revenge,
that the flaw had to be so exquisite, perfected,
minute, unseen and yet visible
it was safe from being detected.
    To this day they don't see it: the flaw is the point.

It's the necessity, it's everything,
the work's lifeless without it. The bruise
on the pear. The planet's wobble. The fungus.
The mutation. The disobedience. The deliberate
    flaw in the Navaho blanket:
                to let the soul out.

Sailing on the Lake of Mars

Emergency Exit signs. Pomegranate wounds.
Clotted canals on chalk eyeballs. Cherries.
Placentas. You'd never think red
could blush, smolder, blaze
through so many shades. Yet it does,

as it shuffles along in the dust,
iron–oxide–rust–rich
even in water thawing on ice
under snow, even here, hidden
beneath the far southern pole:

improbability being the sole
reliable compass on which you can count.
It's a great place however
from which to view clearly
that blue egg, the white-feathered

lapis world where I once lived
—Latitude 40°N Longitude 74°W—
but never quite belonged. There, every step
was swift, heavy. You had to dodge crowds.
The moon, obsessed, never glanced away

even when blind once a month. A year was longer.
So was a day. Here, you weigh less. Each step is
slower. It's colder. It's harder to breathe. There, some
scientists think life may have begun here, then gone
joyriding on a stray asteroid. Maybe

that's how I came here, too—having peeled
away all my selves in the journey
to travel alone and find myself,
know myself, here, back in this bleak
burnt-blood eden, finally home.

This Worthless Act

(for Isel Rivero y Mendes)

This worthless act of poetry, this rhyme,
these empty gestures, this metaphor
is useless as a blind man to a mime,
as futile as a sinking semaphore.

The world's at war again. Refugees swarm
the borders, children wail, men rage, and women weep.
Too little has changed too slowly while the dream
of peace turned nightmare in our sleep.

Before such suffering, well-meant mercies burn
away, leaving us mute to trace the signs
of dreary, tiresome grief. We do not learn.
We just bear witness like these helpless lines

echoing faint messages as indistinct
as ghostly melodies of songbirds long extinct.

The Winter Solstice

These small hours of a slowly dying year
leak through night's cracks—pale, splintery,
bleak. No window's warmth, no gleam, no wintery
cheer shimmers at us. We crawl by in despair,

weary of weeping yet wary of growing numb,
seeing a world doomed by our filth and rage,
suspecting nothing we now grieve can gauge
the final conflagration yet to come.

Like children begging for another chance, some
claim to acquire night vision and to see
bright blurs of hope through the debris
—phosphorescent algae astride seafoam—
until that beauty, these glowing pearls of pus,
reveals the true catastrophe is us.

Necropolitans

In certain cities, the poor don't live in slums
or ghettos, but in the necropolis, city of the dead,
of sunken graves and those above-ground
where floods are common; whole neighborhoods
with mass paupers' pits, middle-class tombstones,
or for the rich, crypts, statuary, mausoleums.

Coming from the airport, you drive through miles
of Cairo's vast necropolis, ancient and modern sprawl alike.
Mexico City is flecked with them, and Metro Manila.
Egypt's great necropolis once housed thousands of slaves
to build the pyramids: skilled masons, architects,
physicians, cooks, priests, embalmers.

These days, necropolitans go about their lives, returning
home from begging or from a day-job like camel-tending
for the tourist rides, wending their way
between the headstones, women lugging groceries
onto improvised shelves inside the catafalques,
while children run and laugh around the graves,

and lovers seek privacy inside sepulchers
of families who boast formidable tombs.
They eat and drink, and they have sex among the dead,
thinking nothing of it. Why should they? Don't we
do it all the time? Eat, drink, make love, here
among the dying? In Mexico, the Day of the Dead

draws people to the cemetery to share picnics, reminisce
with family ghosts, suck sugar skeletons and candy skulls.
In Manila, they sing to the dead. Being a necropolitan
is not so unfamiliar, after all. The notion you might kick aside
a small bone, looking to be human, dislodged from someone
somewhere; or cock your head in pity at a tablet

that grieves a child clipped at the stem of her blossoming
loveliness, only age 12—gestures as lightly preoccupied
as living itself is. And all the while, a drum's slow silent pound
tolls its dirge beneath you like an underground river
whose currents pulse incessant as it flows toward
emptying into an omnivorous sea.

Simple Choices

You want to live forever? Be a god.
Hide the evil in the good,
split the atom from the Id.
Stagger through the darkening wood
passing yourself, lie by lie.

You want to stay hidden? Be a thorn.
Whatever touches you, make it bleed,
mangle it, strangle it, freeze it with scorn.
Stab at the shadows in your need
to miss who casts them or discover why.

You want to play dead? Well, look alive.
Who has given you this day
your daily dread? Dare then to save yourself,
dare risk the dark, dare disobey,
dare perilously live, until you safely die.

III.
WINNOWING

The Last Door

Preparing for her final retrospective at the Whitney Museum in
1970, Georgia O'Keeffe revisited elemental motifs, even as macular
degeneration initiated loss of all but her peripheral vision. Between
1952–1954 she finished an oil-on-canvas titled 'My Last Door'.

Leave it at the gate before you board,
as in an airport when by mistake you packed
your Swiss army knife. Confiscated. No longer
can you be ready for anything now. Leave

it all behind, bit by bit, you'll have no need of any
of it. Now you have peripheral vision only. Like prey.
Zebras, gazelles, all wear eyes set on the side.
Predators' eyes are set straight ahead. You see,

though, into corners. Work one color at a time.
First, master grey. "Nothing is less real
than realism … only by selection, emphasis,
do we approach the real."

You also wrote: "The meaning of a word
is not as exact as the meaning of a color.
Color and shapes make a more definite statement
than words." I'd argue with that

except that color, like music, needs
no translation. Peering at the world aslant
you pierce directly to the heart of vision.
No approximation. No distraction. No illusion.

Watching the tedium of grey flake toward splendor,
you learn patience. What lies in front of you
dizzies to a blur—until you turn your head
sideways to look forward.

The Other Side

(for Blake)

I will know nothing.
I will be ignorant of everything. I will not know
a spoon, a mountain, a war, a star, a word
in any language. I will not know what I do not know.
I will know no one.

Neither will I know innocence, experience, grief,
laughter, fear. I will not know rain plashing softly,
snowfall's whisper, a blue geranium. There will be no
history. I will not know the way cream blooms in coffee.
I will not know poetry.

I will not mourn lovers, or know why babies die,
comprehend the feel of joy, or corduroy, or pain. I will
not know the song of the lark ascending or the garnet
taste of a plum or the concept of quantum entanglement.
I will not know myself.

Odd, then, to trust—while open to this blankness,
this nothingness, this void so utter—that if,
across infinity, blood cries out to blood
decades from now, once you too will know nothing,
the eyelids of my lidless eyes might flutter.

Icicles of Brine

Brine icicles are downward-growing hollow tubes of ice enclosing
plumes of brine. Sometimes called icicles of death, these tendrils can
leak from sea ice near east Antarctica. Ephemeral and seldom seen,
brinicles form when trapped super-cold brine escapes from the ice and
freezes less salty sea water.

—BASED ON REPORTS IN THE GUARDIAN

Soon tearless, I've used them up,
shed my share in mourning,
spilled them for joy, lavished
them on blood kin, lovers,
and a dramatic virtuoso repertoire
of pain, risking dry-eyed clarity,
wrung out, about done now.

I'm keeping a few in reserve,
for the goodbyes, perhaps—but would loathe
getting morbid. Grief for humanity's lives?
Plenty, but that dries up fast. The planet?
Maybe. It won't really matter: earth dives
into sun, sun crisps, universe drifts apart
across widening winters of eternal night.

So that leaves brinicles
trapped in an ice denser than salt,
rare, seldom seen. Until they leak.
It's the curiosity that drags you back,
the treacherous breath promising warmth,
the cosmos newborn, the relenting restart.
It's the thaw that annihilates the heart.

Three Variations in A Minor Key

1. Waltz

Our noisy years seem moments in the being
of the eternal silence ...

—WILLIAM WORDSWORTH

Remember the noisy years, the years
     when I was never sure
     when you were never
     I was never
     we could not be sure if I was
          hearing you, or you were hearing me?

And such a busyness! such
     movement such a
     jockeying for place,
     such going and doing
     saying and rushing everywhere every-
          thing filled with purpose and with price.

Some days survival was challenging.
     Jobs, poems, freelance, rage,
     famine, feast, primary colors
     saffron clamor, magenta demonstrations,
     jail cigarettes brandy silence tears
          I was afraid our noisy years

might never pass, so filled were they
    with phone calls, hurrying, travels,
    shouts, quarrels, sulks,
    and reconciliations.
    But during this a child grew.
        A boy. A lad. A youth. A man. A life.

You're dead now. I inhabit my own quietude
    pre-silence. Meanwhile he
    emails, texts, tours, conferences, braving
    his noisy years with gusto. I watch, in awe
    of him—past envy, pity, or disdain.
        But not for the world would I go back again.

2. Etude

She wore no face here
there was no place here
there'll be no grace here
for such as her,
who never knew hunger
till others were fed
who could not distinguish
the quick from the dead
who pounded herself
into poems till she bled
across dawn, a closed
wound, all the while
boasting I'm fine,
just a mutant, mute,
lone lamentation
mouthed by a deaf world, I'm fine.

3. Nocturne

let the ground quake
let the winds scream
let the storm break
let the rains stream

let the night break
let the dark rise
keep me awake
till the day dies

     why stay awake
     only to weep
     why not let the world break
     on the smooth rocks of sleep

no, while dead stars still streak
through sentient skies
oh keep me awake
as the light dies

The Old Woman Is Talking with Death

Weary of writing about you aslant:
one eye closed, one ear listening, only one
consciousness tuned. Poems about aging, disease,
disability. Euphemisms. All of them poems about you.

> *That's natural, child*, laughs Death, *I'm drawing near.*

You go to hell. Life's full of you these days:
whole species go extinct, the planet gasps,
bumble bees die, redwoods loom swaddled in tin foil
against wildfires; blue whales keen to each other across

poisons through which they swim. Why mourn
humanity's tedious terminal fever? Who'll miss us? More
than a quadrillion quadrillion individual viruses live

on this planet—there are fewer stars in the universe—who
are *you* betting on? Take that, dear first responders.

> *It's normal to feel this way, child*, says Death.

Damn normal! What do I *do*?
Merely thank those who left sentences
for me to climb, rungs in this quaint lost art some call poetry?

> *Child? Child, I'm here.*

It's the laughter. I'm seeking the smile, you know?
Something bleakly comedic: like finding myself
not so sharp anymore, a stooped, slow old lady
bobbling along with her cane, not the slender
strong woman striding through life in her boots.

How you do go on, child.

Alright, yes, I confess I love words … Odd, isn't it?
The two of us, talking as if we were just—

—and who's more delusional, dear?

Oh, decidedly me. The young me could never have
looked you straight in the eye.

But you can. Why didn't you grasp me till now?
Couldn't you see I'm an old woman, too?

I just … never thought of that.

Failure of the imagination?

Maybe. Though it does change everything. No skeleton.
No scythe

—no apocalypse or vengeance.

No vengeance, yes! Or hell, or heaven. Still, you must
admit that Death is cruel.

Cruel? It's Life that's cruel, if you're paying attention.

…

I thought I was. But perhaps that's true.

> *It's why I invented god, you know. Life was too merciless to bear as a Void. Children need toys.*

Toys! We need toys?

> *Not my fault how god got used—gods were meant to play-act little dramas, not inflict meaning! Symbols, so the children could pretend they'd live forever.*

Why was that a good thing?

> *It wasn't. Never is. But they were so terribly afraid of me, you see.*

It must be hard on you, Death. To always feel unwelcome everywhere.

> *Not hard at all. You'd be surprised. The old, the ill, those in unrelenting pain, or in despair. And of course the poets, the mad, the newborn …*

They see you as you really are?

> *Oh, child. They see me as a thousand faces, call me by a million names, from Thanatos to Entropy. But some do see me as the old woman you are.*

The old woman *I* am ... but then if you are ... if I ...
then there is nothing to fear, is there?

I've never been able to find it, if it exists.

But this is great good news. We must tell the world!

No one will believe you, child. No one ever has.

Oh ... pity.

Yes. Pity.

And I wanted to ask you so many things.

Well, you can always—

I think I don't need to, now.

I'm glad you see that. It makes me smile.

There! There it is—there's the smile. Why, you're ...
you're beautiful. Well, then . . .

Well, then.

I don't know how to end our conversation

I do, Death says.

Certain Evenings

We sat in the darkening garden lit
by candleflame and fireflies. The round wood
table drew us in. We weren't wealthy, but we were
content. We ate seafood, roast vegetables, salad
crisp with herbs from the garden—mint, basil, sorrel.
We drank, we laughed; we talked of poetry, films,
music, politics. The birds chanted vespers. We
were three people alive in a time of planetary grief,
three artists trying to live clearly and die well.

You really can't ask more than that. Or less.
If someday in a future unimagined
you sit in such a garden at such an hour
perhaps you might remember us, who went
before, who found some way some time
somehow not to despair, some means
to make things beautiful
and to make beautiful things.
We passed this way.

Falling Awake

It will take you by surprise: *I'm sorry. It's*
stage four. Or: *Watch out—the bus!* Or even just:
She fell, she's bleeding! It will daze you, slink
up on you, like Sunday mornings. You'll think

Oh! But I didn't finish … whatever it was
you'll never think or finish now. If readiness is all,
we should revere it with precision, insist
that for some shocks, readiness does not exist.

Birth. Death. The Mysteries. For such
impossibilities, readiness is nothing —
or it's for princes' grandeur, not the rest
of us. But there'll be wonder in the nest,

the way amorphous albumin and gluey
yoke congeal, then flicker an urge to peck and
peck until resistance cracks with light,
with air that hurts to breathe, and appetite

drives you blind shrieking compelled forward
to a feathered smell, moist, pungent, a hysteria
of gullets, a beak that stuffs your gagging till
full, you gulp and swallow sleep. Meanwhile,

unconcerned, life wheels wide, wild, and awake,
as you, cupped by tender claws, dream on
of readiness circling to dive with folded wings
that spread to seize and bear you outward as it sings.

Other books by Robin Morgan

Dark Matter: New Poems

I've planted myself in the audience
as the patsy I dare to decipher my tricks—
safe I can never see through me.
The Magician and The Magician's Assistant—
I've been both for so long ...
from here on in, all that's left is the magic.

In this major new book of poems, her seventh, Robin Morgan rewards us with the award-winning mastery we've come to expect from her poetry. Her gaze is unflinching, her craft sharp, her mature voice rich with wry wit, survived pain, and her signature chord: an indomitable celebration of life. This powerful collection contains the now-famous poems Morgan reads in her TED Talk—viewed online more than a million times and translated into 24 languages.
   Dark Matter is an unforgettable book.

In *Dark Matter,* her seventh poetry collection, Morgan cannily exploits poetry's ability to be both metaphoric and direct. The voice is often conversational and anecdotal, at other times it is layered and allusive. What drives the collection is a deep and passionate intensity, which only a life spent in endless interrogation and interaction with self and world can achieve and sustain.
                    —Patricia Skyes, *Live Encounters*

Her love for poetry inspires a beautiful sense of wonder and awe in this poet and ignites a fire in the feminist in us all. *Dark Matter* by Robin Morgan is an absolute masterpiece and should be shared with everyone willing to listen.
                    —Nik Shone, *Other Terrain*

ISBN: 9781925581430

Parallax: A Novel

She inspected her knitting. "A yarn imagines itself, you know," she murmured," from separate strands. Every story is made of strands, too, of worlds that keep unfolding simultaneously along the same yarn. You can spot one at a time or, rarely, a multitude swarming—though no yarner can ever glimpse both the individual tale and the swarm at the same moment. Imagination can conceal while it reveals. Sooner or later, though, everything gets used."

In *Parallax*, Robin Morgan's most radiant prose, spare but sensuous, welcomes you into her dazzling imagination. This is a story about storytelling—a set of shorter tales which, like Russian dolls, nest and fit together to reveal a larger one.

A fable for the future, a prediction about the past, *Parallax* is a luscious story that enfolds you and demands immediate rereading the moment you finish, a story that surprises you and invites you to play with the patterns inside its paradoxes, a story whose characters will accompany you for the rest of your life.

The more I read, the more I did not want to stop, I loved the mixture of frame and stories … the good-natured tone, the wit, the generosity. This is vintage Morgan.

—Ursula K. Le Guin

I loved the timeless folktale feel of the stories, and the wonderful evocation of the lives of Monarch butterflies, and the quiet, domestic humility and contradictions of The Yarner and the stranger. I cannot pretend to know how to definitively explain the "meaning" of all of the stories *Parallax* contains, but I think this is the point. They are stories about learning to see enormity and complexity and striving to arrive at a balanced perspective on all the world's shiftiness and change. It is a book that will surely make readers think, but is also a tale told masterfully: full of hooks and needles.

—Daniela Brozek Cordier, *Plumwood Mountain Journal*

ISBN: 9781925581959

*If you would like to know more about
Spinifex Press, write to us for a free catalogue, visit our
website or email us for further information
on how to subscribe to our monthly newsletter.*

Spinifex Press
PO Box 105
Mission Beach QLD 4852
Australia

www.spinifexpress.com.au
women@spinifexpress.com.au